Tales of King Arthur

Retold by David Foulds

OXFORD
UNIVERSITY PRESS

OXFORD
UNIVERSITY PRESS

Oxford University Press is a department of the University of Oxford.
It furthers the University's objective of excellence in research, scholarship,
and education by publishing worldwide in

Oxford New York

Athens Auckland Bangkok Bogotá Buenos Aires Calcutta
Cape Town Chennai Dar es Salaam Delhi Florence Hong Kong Istanbul
Karachi Kuala Lumpur Madrid Melbourne Mexico City Mumbai
Nairobi Paris São Paulo Shanghai Singapore Taipei Tokyo Toronto Warsaw

with associated companies in Berlin Ibadan

Oxford is a registered trade mark of Oxford University Press

© Oxford University Press 1994

First published 1994

This impression (lowest digit)

5 7 9 11 10 8 6 4

Retold by David Foulds

Illustrated by Steve Worthington

Syllabus designer: David Foulds

Text processing and analysis by Luxfield Consultants Ltd

ISBN 0 19 586306 2

Printed in Hong Kong
Published by Oxford University Press (China) Ltd
18th Floor, Warwick House East, Taikoo Place, 979 King's Road, Quarry Bay
Hong Kong

TALES OF KING ARTHUR

The *Oxford Progressive English Readers* series provides a wide range of reading for learners of English.

Each book in the series has been written to follow the strict guidelines of a syllabus, wordlist and structure list. The texts are graded according to these guidelines; Grade 1 at a 1,400 word level, Grade 2 at a 2,100 word level, Grade 3 at a 3,100 word level, Grade 4 at a 3,700 word level and Grade 5 at a 5,000 word level.

The latest methods of text analysis, using specially designed software, ensure that readability is carefully controlled at every level. Any new words which are vital to the mood and style of the story are explained within the text, and reoccur throughout for maximum reinforcement. New language items are also clarified by attractive illustrations.

Each book has a short section containing carefully graded exercises and controlled activities, which test both global and specific understanding.

CONTENTS

1 THE FORGOTTEN SWORD   1

2 THE NEW KING   7

3 THE FIGHT BY THE FOUNTAIN   13

4 THE ROUND TABLE   19

5 THE KNIGHT OF THE TWO SWORDS   25

6 THE KNIGHT WHO DESTROYED A CASTLE   30

7 SIR LAUNCELOT AND SIR TURQUIN   36

8 A DAY OF MIRACLES   41

9 THE TWO ROADS   46

10 SIR GALAHAD, KNIGHT OF THE GRAIL   52

11 THE WICKED SIR MORDRED   58

12 THE DEATH OF KING ARTHUR   64

QUESTIONS AND ACTIVITIES   70

CONTENTS

THE FORGOTTEN SWORD

The sword in the stone

When King Uther Pendragon died, the kingdom of Britain fell into great danger. For a long time there was no king. Instead, the great lords fought with one another. Many of them wanted to be king, but not one 5 of them was stronger than all the others. Everywhere they argued among themselves about their lands and many other things. Everywhere there were battles and small wars. For a long time there was no peace in the land. 10

Then Merlin, the strange old enchanter, came to London. He came to see the Bishop. He asked the Bishop to send a message to all the lords.

'Tell them to come to London at Christmas,' said Merlin. 'Tell them they must come to a great meeting 15 here, in the abbey church. We shall all kneel down together and pray to God. We shall ask Him, by some miracle, to help us find the true King of Britain.'

The Bishop did as Merlin asked.

On Christmas Day, the lords of Britain, their ladies, 20 and many ordinary people, met together in the greatest of all the churches in old London. There, all day long, they prayed. They asked God for a miracle. They asked God to show them who the new King of Britain would be. 25

In the evening, when the prayers were finished, the people looked up and saw something strange. Near the high altar stood a great stone. It had not been there before.

It was of bright,
white marble. Set hard
in the centre was a large,
heavy anvil of grey steel. Stuck in the
5   anvil, point down, was a sharp sword.

The people were surprised and excited when they saw this. It was a miracle. They went to look at this strange sight. When they got closer, they saw the sword had gold writing on it. It said:

'HE WHO PULLS THIS SWORD FROM THE ANVIL *5* IN THE STONE IS THE TRUE KING OF ALL THIS LAND.'

Some great lords immediately pushed themselves to the front of the crowd. They stood before the marble stone and the great steel anvil. They took hold of the *10* sword, and tried to pull it out. But not one of them could move it. It was stuck fast.

'The man who will have the sword is not here,' said the Bishop. 'But I am sure God will bring him here soon.' He made the lords choose ten good knights to *15* stay by the stone day and night until the man who would be king was found.

The Bishop did not want the great lords to leave London. He wanted them to be there when God showed them the new king. So he arranged that one *20* week later, on New Year's Day, there should be great games, or a tournament, outside the city walls. There would be competitions and fights between the best lords and the strongest knights. No one would want to leave London if there was going to be a tournament. *25*

Sir Kay needs his sword

On New Year's Day, after going to church, everyone went out to the place where the tournament would *30* be held. The roads and fields all around London were filled with happy, excited people. There were knights riding great, fierce war-horses. Some had come to joust; they would take part in fights with other knights to see who was the bravest and best. *35*

The knights wore bright armour. Some had come
to take part in competitions and watch the
tourneys, when many lords and knights
all fought together at the same time.

5   The lords brought tents
made of bright-coloured silks with them.
Their servants set the tents up at the sides of
the fields. With the lords came their ladies, wearing
beautiful dresses and fine jewellery. Everywhere the
10   ordinary people came from London and the villages
around, wearing their best clothes. They came out for
a day's holiday, and to enjoy the tournament.

Among the people riding to the tournament was an old knight called Sir Ector. He owned lands and farms near London, and was quite rich. Sir Ector was too old to take part in the tournament. He had just come to watch. But with him rode two younger men. One was Sir Kay, who had only just been made a knight. The other, younger man, was Arthur. Arthur was not old enough to be a knight. He had come to help Sir Kay, and to watch him take part. Sir Kay would be fighting in the jousts for the first time in his life, and both young men were very excited.

As they were riding to the tournament, Sir Kay suddenly stopped.

'My sword,' he said, looking around. 'Arthur, I don't believe it! I have forgotten to bring my sword!'

The younger man searched for the sword among the things they had brought with them. It was not there.

Arthur knew how important it was for Sir Kay to have his sword. 'I will go back and get it, Sir Kay,' he said. Before anyone could stop him, he rode off as fast as he could. But when he got home, there was no one there. Everyone had gone out to watch the tournament. The place was locked up, and Arthur could not get in.

Arthur's idea

Arthur could not get Sir Kay's sword, but he knew he had to do something. Then he had an idea. He remembered Sir Ector had spoken about a sword in the abbey church. Arthur could not remember everything Sir Ector had said, because he had not been listening carefully. But he thought the sword might still be there. He said to himself, 'Sir Kay cannot be without a sword for the tournament. I will ride to the abbey church, and take the sword that is set in the stone.'

Arthur rode back to London quickly. When he reached the abbey church, he jumped off his horse, tied it to the gate-post, and ran inside. There was no one at all in the great old building. Everyone had gone to
5 the tournament.

There, by the high altar, Arthur saw the white marble stone, and the grey steel anvil, and the sword with the words written on it. He did not stop to read what the writing said. There was no time. Arthur just walked
10 straight up to the stone, took the sword from the anvil, and left. Shouting to everyone to get out of his way, he rode, quick as the wind, back to Sir Kay, and gave the sword to him.

When Sir Kay saw the sword, he knew what it was.
15 He had listened carefully to Sir Ector, though he had not really believed him. Now he thought the story of the sword in the stone must be completely untrue. If young Arthur could pull it out, then anyone could!

He rode to Sir Ector, his father, and said, laughing,
20 'Look at this, sir! I have the sword from the stone. Will you say that I am the true King of Britain, now?'

When Sir Ector saw the sword, he did not laugh. He looked surprised, and serious. He had been in the abbey church when some of the great lords had tried
25 to pull the sword from the stone. He knew them. They were not just important people: they were great fighting men, and very strong. They wanted to be king. They would not pretend that they could not pull it out.

'Give the sword to me,' said Sir Ector. 'We must take
30 it back to the church immediately.'

'But the tournament...' said Sir Kay and Arthur together.

'Come with me, both of you,' said Sir Ector. From the sound of his voice, they knew better than to argue with
35 him.

THE NEW KING

Sir Ector explains

At the abbey church they all got off their horses and went inside. The place was still empty. It was a large, dark, quiet place. There was no other building in the whole kingdom as big as this. Now that he was no longer in a hurry, Arthur felt strange being in such a large building, with no one else there.

Sir Ector walked straight to the marble stone.

'Now, tell me again,' he said to Sir Kay, 'how did you get this sword?'

'Sir,' said Sir Kay, 'my brother, Arthur, brought it to me.'

'Arthur?' Sir Ector could not believe what he was hearing. 'How did you get this sword, Arthur?' he asked.

Arthur thought he had done something wrong. He knew he must tell the complete truth. 'Sir,' he said, 'there was no one at home when I went back for my brother's sword. They had all gone to watch the jousts. The house was locked, and I could not get in. I thought my brother, Sir Kay, could not take part in the jousts without a sword, so I came here and pulled this one from the stone. No one saw me do it. I can return it when the jousts are finished.'

'Weren't there any knights standing by the sword?' asked Sir Ector.

'No, sir,' Arthur replied.

'Now,' said Sir Ector to Arthur. 'I have something serious to say to you. If what you have told me is the truth, then you must be king of this land.'

'Me?' said Arthur. 'But why must I be king?'

'Because that is what God wants,' said Sir Ector. 'Only one man in the whole world can pull this sword from the stone. That man is the true king of this land. Now let me see if you can put the sword back, and then pull it out again.'

'That is easy,' said Arthur. He put the sword into the anvil. But before he could pull it out again, Sir Ector stopped him. Instead, the old knight tried to pull the sword out of the stone himself. He could not move it.

'You try,' Sir Ector said to Sir Kay. Sir Kay stepped forward. He pulled at the sword with all his strength; but still the sword did not move.

'And now you, Arthur,' said Sir Ector.

'Yes, sir,' said Arthur. The sword came out easily.

Then Sir Ector immediately knelt down on the ground in front of Arthur, and so did Sir Kay.

Arthur was astonished. 'Oh no,' he said, 'my own dear father! My dear brother! Why are you kneeling to me?'

'My Lord Arthur,' said Sir Ector, 'you do not know the whole truth. I was never your father. I am not even sure who your family is. I have always believed you were the child of a good family, but now I see you come from a much greater family than I thought.' 5

Then Sir Ector told Arthur how, many years before, the enchanter, Merlin, had come to his house. He had brought a baby boy with him, and asked him and his wife to look after the child. That baby was Arthur. Ever since, Arthur had lived with Sir Ector as his younger 10 son.

Arthur cried when he understood that Sir Ector was not his real father. He loved both Sir Ector and Sir Kay very much.

Then they all went to the Bishop. They told him how 15 the sword had been pulled from the stone, and by whom. When the Bishop saw Arthur, and how young he was, he was very surprised.

At the feast of Pentecost

After the tournament, a great many lords and knights 20 came back to the abbey church. Some of them tried to take the sword from the stone, but Arthur was the only person who could pull it out.

Many lords were angry about this. They said it was a great shame to them, and to the kingdom, to have a 25 boy as their king. They said that Arthur did not even come from a family of kings. They asked the Bishop to wait for a month before he made Arthur king. Then all the lords would meet at the abbey church, and try to pull the sword from the stone again. 30

A month later, many more great lords came and tried to win the sword, but none succeeded. Arthur pulled the sword from the stone easily, just as before.

The lords were still unhappy. They asked the Bishop to do nothing until Easter. At Easter, when exactly the same thing happened, the lords asked the Bishop to wait for another six weeks, until the feast of Pentecost.

At Pentecost, more people came to the abbey church than ever before. All the greatest lords and all the strongest knights in the kingdom were there. All who wished, tried to pull the sword from the stone, but Arthur was still the only one who could do it. He did it again and again, in front of all the people, rich and poor, important people and ordinary people.

At last the people shouted out together, 'We want Arthur to be our king. We can see that this is what God is telling us. We will not make Arthur wait any longer.'

They knelt down, and cried to Arthur not to be angry for making him wait so long. Arthur forgave them. He took the great sword in his hands, and placed it on the high altar. Then the Bishop brought a golden crown and placed it on Arthur's head. He took Arthur by the hand, and made him stand in front of the people. Britain had a new king.

Then Merlin came and told the great lords and all the people who Arthur really was. He said the baby boy he had left with Sir Ector and his wife was really the child of Uther Pendragon and the Lady Igrayne. Arthur had come from a family of kings. He was the son of one of the greatest kings of Britain. 5

The court at Camelot

Arthur was a good king, strong and brave, true and just. In a few years the land was at peace once more. His palace was not at London, but at Winchester, which in those days was called Camelot. 10

As the years went by, many knights came to Camelot. He welcomed them all. He made the bravest and the best his own, special knights. These he sent out on journeys, or quests. He sent them to fight against wickedness and evil, and to do what was right and good. Above all, he ordered these great, strong fighters, to be merciful to their enemies, and to respect women and those weaker than themselves. At the great feasts of Christmas, Easter and Pentecost, the knights would return to Camelot, and tell the king of their adventures. After Arthur had chosen his queen, the knights were known as 'the Knights of the Round Table.' 15 20

Of all the people at the court, the one King Arthur spoke to most often was Merlin. Merlin was a man who knew magic. He had strange powers. At any time, he could make himself look different, so that when people saw him, they did not know who he was. He could disappear quite suddenly, and, a short time later, reappear somewhere else many miles away. He could see into the future. 25 30

Merlin was at Camelot, with the king, for many years. Whenever King Arthur needed help, Merlin was there.

THE FIGHT BY THE FOUNTAIN

Riding towards death

King Arthur was angry. One of his young knights, Sir Griflet, had been badly wounded in a fight.

'A knight has put up a tent by a fountain in the forest,' Sir Griflet had said. 'He sits outside his tent, and makes all the knights that go past joust with him. He is a big, powerful man. No one can beat him.'

Next morning, as soon as it was light, the king put on his armour, climbed onto his horse, and rode off to look for Sir Griflet's enemy.

The king rode through the green forest all morning. For some time he met no one. Then, about the middle of the morning, he saw some people in the road in front of him. There were three strong, rough-looking men chasing an old man. They looked like robbers. They caught the old man. It seemed they were going to kill him.

'Stop that!' the king shouted out, very loudly. He made his horse run forward. He lowered his long sharp spear, and rode towards them hard and fast.

The three men turned and saw an armed knight charging towards them on a great war-horse. They let the old man go. They ran away as fast as they could.

Arthur stopped by the old man. It was Merlin.

'Oh Merlin,' said Arthur, 'you know many things, but you would have died if I had not been here.'

'I could have saved myself if I had wanted to,' said Merlin with a strange look on his face. 'You are much closer to death, now, than I was then.'

Arthur smiled and helped the old enchanter onto his horse. Merlin often said strange things that he did not understand. The two of them rode on together.

A great fighter

5 After they had ridden for a short while, the king and Merlin came to a place where there was a cool fountain, glittering in the sunlight. By the fountain was a tent, made of rich, brightly-coloured silks. Sitting in a chair, in front of the tent, was a big, powerful-looking knight.
10 He was wearing his armour, and ready to fight. It was Sir Griflet's enemy.

'Sir knight,' Arthur called out, 'why do you make all the knights who come past joust with you?'

'I do it because I like doing it,' replied the knight. 'I
15 have always done it. I always will. It is my custom.'

'Then I will change your custom,' said Arthur.

'And I shall not let you,' said the knight. The knight got up, picked up his shield, took hold of a very long, sharp spear, and got on his horse. Immediately, the two charged towards one another.

Arthur rode towards the knight; the knight rode towards Arthur. Each man made his horse go faster and faster. When they were close, they lowered their spears. Then, with a great crash, they came together. The king's spear broke against the knight's shield. The knight's spear broke against the king's shield. Arthur immediately pulled out his sword.

'No, wait,' said the knight; 'not swords. It is better to run together again with sharp spears.'

'But I have no other spear,' said Arthur.

'I have plenty,' said the knight. He called to his servant to bring out two good spears. Arthur took one and the knight took the other.

They rode away from one another for a distance. Then both turned to face each other. They lowered their spears and rode forwards hard and fast. When they came together for the second time, there was another great crash. Again, both spears broke against the shields. Immediately Arthur pulled out his sword.

'No,' said the knight, 'I have never met anyone as good at jousting as you. Let us joust once more.'

'Very well,' said Arthur.

The servant brought out two more spears, and for the third time they ran together. This time Arthur's spear broke, but the knight's did not. The knight's spear hit the king so hard in the middle of his shield that the king, and his horse, fell to the ground.

Arthur was not hurt. Immediately he jumped up, and pulled out his sword. This time the knight got off his horse. Holding his shield in front of him, he ran at Arthur.

Then began a great battle. Again and again, both men lifted their swords into the air. They smashed them down on each other. They cut into each other's shields so much that pieces of wood and metal flew through the air. Then the knight's sword hit against the king's sword, and broke it in two. Arthur had no sword. The knight said, 'Now, if you do not surrender to me, you will die.'

5   'Stop what you are doing, sir knight,' Merlin shouted. 'If you kill your enemy, you will put this kingdom in great danger.'

'Why, who is he?' asked the knight.

'He is Arthur, the king,' said Merlin, coming closer.
10   He took hold of the knight's arm, and immediately the knight fell onto the ground in a deep sleep. Then Merlin helped Arthur onto his horse, and they rode away.

'What have you done, Merlin?' said Arthur. 'Have you used your magic to kill this good knight? What a great
15   fighter he was. I wish he were still alive.'

'He is just asleep,' said Merlin. 'He will wake up in three hours' time.' Then he looked at Arthur. 'I told you you were going towards your death,' he added. 'You are strong and brave, but you would have died if I had
20   not been here.'

The magic sword

They rode further into the forest until they came to a wide lake. The water there was as smooth as a mirror. All around were tall hills and dark woods. It was very
25   quiet. Arthur remembered how he had felt in the abbey church, when he, Sir Ector, and Sir Kay were the only three people in that large old building. He felt the same now, standing by this quiet lake, with no one there except himself and Merlin.

30   'Look,' said Merlin softly, pointing to the middle of the lake.

Arthur looked. His eyes opened wide with surprise. His blood ran cold. There, a long way out in the lake,

an arm had risen from
the water. In its hand was a
bright shining sword. The arm did
not move. It was as still as stone.

Then Arthur noticed someone walking
slowly along the side of the lake, coming towards
them. It was a woman, beautifully dressed in fine
clothes. 'Who is this?' Arthur whispered.

'It is the Lady of the Lake,' said Merlin. 'She is a great
enchantress. The lake and all the land around is hers. 10
When she comes near, ask her about the sword.'

'My Lady,' said Arthur, when the lady came closer, 'what sword is that, that the arm is holding? I wish it were mine, for I have no sword.'

'King Arthur,' said the lady, 'the sword is mine. If you will give me a gift when I ask it, you may have the sword.'

'I will give you anything,' said Arthur.

The lady seemed pleased. She smiled. 'Very well,' she said. 'There is a boat hidden further along the shore. Get into it, row out into the lake, and take the sword from the arm. I will ask for my gift later.'

Arthur and Merlin tied their horses to two trees, and went to look for the boat. They soon found it. They got in and rowed out across the smooth grey water of the lake. When they came to the sword, Arthur took it by the handle. Immediately the hand let go, and the arm went softly down under the water.

'The name of the sword is Excalibur,' said Merlin. 'It is a magic sword. It will cut through metal. No other sword in the world can break it.' Arthur kept the sword for the rest of his life.

THE ROUND TABLE

Princess Guenevere

One day King Arthur said to Merlin, 'My lords will give me no peace. They are always telling me that I must marry.'

'Is there any lady that you love more than another?' 5 asked Merlin.

'I love Guenevere, the beautiful daughter of King Leodegrance,' the king replied; 'this lady is the loveliest lady that I have ever met.'

'Sir,' said Merlin, 'she is one of the fairest women 10 alive. But if you didn't love her so much, I would find you another. I know of one who is beautiful and good, and who would please you much more. But if your heart is set on Guenevere, you will not want to think of anyone else.' 15

Then Merlin went to talk to King Leodegrance. He told him that the king wanted to marry his daughter.

King Leodegrance was very pleased. 'For a wedding present,' he said, 'I shall send him the Round Table. It has places for 150 knights. I can let him have one 20 hundred of my own good knights, but I do not have the full number. So many have been killed.'

Soon afterwards, Merlin took Guenevere and the Round Table with the one hundred knights, to Camelot. They all travelled together, by water and by land. The 25 ladies had on their most colourful dresses. The knights wore armour that they had cleaned until it glittered brightly in the spring sunlight. Happily they went on the long journey, on horseback and by boat, to King Arthur's court. 30

The king was very happy when he saw Guenevere and the Round Table. He said, 'I have loved this beautiful lady for many years. She is the ruler of my heart. And these knights with the Round Table please me more than all the gold in the world.' Then the king asked the Bishop to get everything ready for the wedding.

'Now, Merlin,' said Arthur, 'there is something I want you to do. Go through all this land and find me fifty of the bravest, best, most honourable men in the kingdom. Then the Round Table will be complete, with its 150 good knights.'

Within a short time Merlin had found twenty-eight. He said the other places should be left empty, for brave knights who might come later.

Then a great feast was made ready. The wedding of the king to the beautiful Lady Guenevere was held in the Church of St Stephen's, at Camelot.

The great stroke

After the wedding, the king and his knights took their places at the Round Table in the great hall. As they sat there, something strange happened. A white deer ran into the hall. Sixty black hunting hounds followed it, making a great noise as they ran. The deer went all the way round the Round Table, and then out of the hall again. The hounds followed.

'Now,' said Merlin to the king, 'let us send one of your young knights on a special quest. Let us ask Sir Gawain to follow the white deer, and bring it back to Camelot.'

Sir Gawain was one of the youngest knights. He was a brave young man, and very pleased to be asked to do something for the king. He took his younger brother, Gaheris, with him.

Before long, the two young men were riding hard through the forest after the white deer. They could not see it, but they knew, from the noise of the hounds, which way to go.

They came to a river. They saw the deer swimming across. Sir Gawain decided to follow. Suddenly, he noticed a tall knight standing on the other side. The knight shouted across, 'Sir, if you want to come over here, you must joust with me.'

'I will do anything I have to do in order to follow my quest,' said Sir Gawain. He and Gaheris made their horses swim across the river.

They soon reached the other side. Then Sir Gawain and the other knight took their spears and rode towards one another as hard as they could. Sir Gawain was the better jouster. He knocked the other knight off his horse. Then Sir Gawain turned his horse and ordered the other knight to surrender.

'No,' said the knight, 'I shall not surrender. You were better than me on horseback, but I ask you, brave knight, to get down and fight me with swords.'

Sir Gawain jumped to the ground. Then both knights held up their shields and hit at each other with their swords. Sir Gawain was very strong. He hit the other knight so hard that his sword cut through the knight's helmet and into his head. Immediately, the knight fell down dead.

'Ah!' said Gaheris, 'that was
5 a great stroke for such
a young knight.'

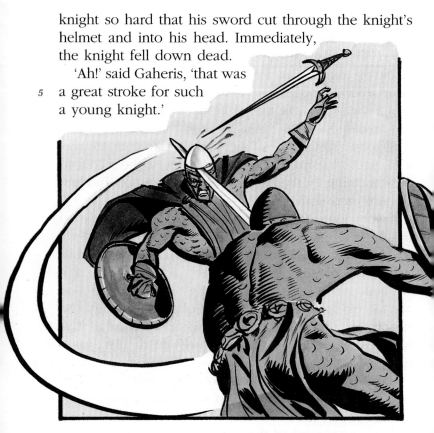

The knight who showed no mercy

Sir Gawain and Gaheris then chased the deer into a castle. Six of the hounds still followed. The hounds
10 began to attack the deer.

Hearing the noise, a knight came out to see what was happening outside. He had a sword in his hand. He immediately killed two of the hounds, and chased the others away. But it was too late to save the white deer.
15 The poor animal was dead.

'Oh my white deer,' said the knight. 'How sad I am that you are dead. My dear lady gave you to me, and

I have not taken good care of you. But now I will punish those who have caused your death.'

The knight went back in, put on his armour, and came out again. When he returned, he saw Sir Gawain standing there. He thought Sir Gawain had let his dogs 5 kill the deer. Without saying a word, he attacked Sir Gawain.

The two knights struck together. They cut into each other's shields. They smashed their swords onto each other's helmets. They hit angrily at each other's armour. 10 They wounded each other until the blood ran down to their feet. At last Sir Gawain hit the knight so hard that he fell. The knight begged Sir Gawain not to kill him. He said he would surrender.

'You will die,' said Sir Gawain, 'for killing the 15 hounds.'

'I will do all I can to make things right,' said the knight.

But Sir Gawain would show him no mercy. He undid the knight's helmet and pulled it off. He lifted his sword 20 high into the air, and was going to cut the knight's head off.

Just then a lady came out of the castle. She saw what was happening. She cried out for mercy, and ran and threw herself across the knight. But she was too 25 late. The great heavy sword came crashing down. Sir Gawain could not stop it. He cut off the lady's head, by accident.

'Alas,' said Gaheris, 'for the rest of your life you will be ashamed of that stroke. You should be merciful to 30 those who ask for mercy. A knight without mercy is without honour.'

Sir Gawain was astonished at the death of this lady. He did not know what to do. He said to the knight, 'Get up. I will give you mercy,' 35

'I want no mercy now,' said the knight. 'You have killed my lady. I loved her more than anything else on earth.'

'It was not my wish to kill her,' said Sir Gawain. 'But now you must go to King Arthur and tell him what has happened. Tell him how you were defeated by the knight that went in the quest of the white deer.'

The following day, Sir Gawain and Gaheris rode back to Camelot. Sir Gawain told the king and queen of his adventures.

When the king and queen heard how the lady was killed, and that this had happened because Gawain would show the knight no mercy, they were very displeased. The queen said that Sir Gawain should have a special quest. She said that for the rest of his life he must take special care of all ladies. He should always be gentle and polite to them. He should always help them when they were in trouble. Most important of all, he should never refuse mercy to anyone who asked, man or woman.

THE KNIGHT OF THE TWO SWORDS

The best knight

One day, at the court at Camelot, a lady came to see King Arthur. While they were talking, Arthur noticed she had a heavy sword around her waist. The king was surprised. 'Lady,' he said, 'why do you carry that sword?'   5

'I wish I were not carrying it,' said the lady, 'but I must carry it until the knight who is the best in all the land draws it from its sheath. So far I have met no knight that can pull it out.'

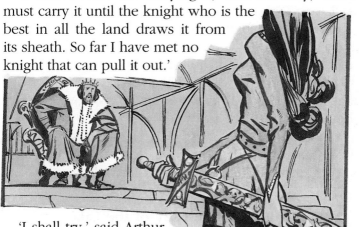

'I shall try,' said Arthur. Then the king took hold of the sheath, and held the sword by its handle. He pulled at it with all his strength, but the sword would not move. Then all the knights of the Round Table that   15 were there tried, one after the other. Not one could pull the sword from its sheath. They were all astonished.

At that time, there was a very poor knight called Balin staying at Camelot. He was not one of those who had a place at the Round Table. However, although he was   20

poor, his heart was good. He heard about the lady and
the sword. He went quietly to the great hall to watch.
As the lady was about to leave, he called out to her,

'My lady,' he said politely, 'please let me try, too. I
5   know I am not well dressed, but I am a brave and
honest knight, and my heart is true.'

The lady looked at the poor knight. 'Very well,' she
said, 'you may try to take the sword, if you can.'

Then Balin took the sword by the handle and drew
10 it out easily.

'This knight must be the best in the land,' said the
lady, turning to the king. 'He will do many great deeds.
And now, gentle knight, please give me my sword
back.'

15 But Balin liked the sword very much. He did not
want to return it. 'No,' he said, 'I will keep the sword,
until someone takes it from me.'

'It would not be wise to keep it,' said the lady. 'With
that sword you will kill the person you love most in
20 the world.'

But Balin would not listen. He kept the sword. And
as he already had a sword of his own, he became
known as 'the Knight of the Two Swords.'

Balin and the Lady of the Lake

25 Soon afterwards, another lady came to the palace. She
was beautifully dressed, and rode on a white horse. She
came into the great hall, and walked up to the king.

'I have come to ask you for a gift,' she said to the
king. 'You promised me one when I gave you the
30 sword, Excalibur.'

It was the Lady of the Lake.

The king was very happy to see her. 'Of course,' he
said. 'Ask for anything you wish.'

'I ask for the head of the knight that won the sword,' said the lady, 'If not that, I would like the head of the lady that brought the sword. Best of all, I would like both their heads, for the knight killed my brother, and the lady caused my father's death.'

'I may not give you either of their heads,' said King Arthur. He was astonished at the lady's words. 'Please ask for something else.'

'There is nothing else I want,' said the lady.

When Balin heard that the Lady of the Lake had come to court, and asked for his head, he immediately knew who she was. The lady was an enchantress, and an old enemy of his family. She had killed his mother. Balin had been searching for her for three years to punish her.

He went straight to the hall. She was still there, talking to the king. 'Oh evil enchantress,' Balin cried out, 'you would have my head, and so you shall lose yours.' With that he took out his sword and, there, in front of the king, he cut off her head.

'Alas, for shame!' said Arthur. 'Why have you done that? You have brought dishonour on me and all my court. I had made a promise to this lady. She came here thinking that she would be safe. I shall never forgive you for killing this lady.'

Balin then told the king how, through her wickedness and lies, she had caused his mother to be burned to death. The king would not listen. He was very angry with Balin. He told Balin to leave Camelot immediately.

Balin and Balan

Balin left Camelot sadly. He was glad the Lady of the Lake was dead, but he was unhappy that King Arthur was so angry.

As he rode through the forest, he met a knight going towards Camelot. It was his brother, Balan, who was on his way to look for him at the court of King Arthur. They had not seen each other for three years, and were
5 very happy.

Balin told his brother what had happened. 'I am sad,' he said, 'that King Arthur is displeased with me. He is the best of all kings. I want to do something so that he will forgive me.'

10 'But what can you do?' asked Balan.

'King Arthur's greatest enemy, King Rience, is not far from here,' said Balin. 'He is going to attack one of King Arthur's castles. Let us go there, as quickly as we can, and see if we can do something for King Arthur.'

15 As they rode through the forest, they met Merlin, who agreed to help them. Merlin made them hide among some small trees beside a narrow road. They waited there until it was almost midnight. Then Merlin told them to make themselves ready. 'King Rience is coming
20 this way with sixty of his best knights,' he said.

'How will we know which one is the king?' asked Balin.

Just then they heard the sound of riders coming.

'Quick,' said Merlin. 'The king is the first one.'

25 As soon as the first rider reached them, Balin and his brother jumped out into the road. They pulled King Rience down from his frightened horse. They knocked him to the ground, and badly wounded him.

Then the king's knights rode up, but the road was
30 narrow. They could not all get close to their king, to help him.

A great battle followed. Standing back to back, the brothers hit out hard at all who came near them. They were both brave knights, and powerful fighters. King
35 Rience's knights did not know who their enemies were.

It was dark, and they could not see easily. They had no idea they were only fighting two men. In the darkness, many of King Rience's knights fought each other. Before long, forty of them lay dead on the ground. After that, the others got back on their horses, and rode away.

Balin and Balan turned back to King Rience. They would have killed him but he asked them to be merciful. The two knights helped the king onto his horse. He was very weak. He rode slowly away through the night.

When they looked for Merlin, they could not find him. Merlin had disappeared. Soon afterwards, he came to King Arthur and told him how his greatest enemy had been attacked and beaten.

'Those are two marvellous knights,' said King Arthur. 'Balin is braver than any man I know. I forgive him for what he did to the Lady of the Lake. I wish that he would stay with me here at Camelot.'

After defeating King Rience, Balin and Balan decided to go different ways to look for more adventures.

THE KNIGHT WHO DESTROYED A CASTLE

The invisible knight

Balin rode through the forest. After an hour or two, he met a knight. Balin stopped to speak to him. As they were talking, they heard the sound of a horse coming
5 towards them. They looked around, but saw nothing. The noise got louder. The horse sounded heavy and powerful. It was charging towards them. Then, when it seemed to be right beside them, the knight screamed out. A great hole appeared in his armour, as if a spear
10 had gone through it. Blood flowed down to the ground. He fell from his horse, badly wounded.

'I have been killed by my enemy,' said the knight. 'His name is Garlon. He can make himself invisible.'

Soon afterwards the knight died. Balin buried him
15 and went on sadly, for the knight was a good man.

As Balin rode on through the forest, he stopped here and there to speak to the people he met. He heard many stories about Garlon. Garlon was a brother of King Pellam. Through his power to make himself
20 invisible, Garlon had killed many good knights. Then Balin heard that King Pellam was going to give a great feast at his castle — Castle Carbonek. Balin thought Garlon might be at the feast, and decided to go himself.

When Balin reached Castle Carbonek, he was taken
25 to the great hall. He sat down among many knights and their ladies. He asked one of them, 'Is there a knight here called Garlon?'

'Over there,' said the knight. 'He is the one with the dark hair.'

Balin wondered what to do. 'If I kill him here,' he thought, 'I shall not be able to leave safely. But if I do nothing, he will kill many more good knights.'

The room in the tower

Garlon saw Balin looking at him. He came over and hit Balin across the face with the back of his hand. 'Don't stare at me like that!' he shouted angrily. 'Just enjoy the feast. Do what you came here to do.'

'Very well,' said Balin, 'I will do what I came to do.' Then he stood up, drew out his sword, smashed it down and cut Garlon's head off.

At once King Pellam stood up. 'Knight, have you killed my brother?' he shouted. 'You shall die for that. I will kill you myself.'

King Pellam took hold of a great battleaxe. He struck eagerly at Balin. Balin put his sword up to stop the axe from cutting him, but the axe was so heavy and the king was so strong that the sword broke.

Balin ran out of the hall, looking for a weapon. He went from room to room, but could see nothing. All the time, King Pellam chased after him.

At last Balin came to a tower. He climbed up the stairs quickly. At the top was a door. He opened it, and went through.

He found himself in a room filled with beautiful things. Fine curtains of many different colours hung around the walls. There was a bed there, covered with the richest cloth of gold you have ever seen. Lying in the bed was
5 a very old man. At the side of the room stood a table of glittering gold with four silver legs. On top of the table was a marvellous spear covered with strange writing.

Balin immediately took hold of the spear. He turned
10 to King Pellam, who had just burst into the room. With all his strength Balin threw the spear straight at the king and wounded him. The king fell down in a faint.

Just then, Balin heard a loud, low rumbling. It grew dark outside. The rumbling grew louder and louder
15 until the whole world was filled with noise, darkness, smoke, and the sound of frightened people screaming. The castle began to shake. All around, walls broke and fell. Balin fell, too, and something heavy fell on him, so that he could not move. The noise and the dust and
20 the darkness were terrifying. Most of the castle fell down. King Pellam and Balin lay there, unable to move, for three days.

Then Merlin came. He helped Balin up. He told him that the spear he had used was a very special one. It
25 had great power. When Balin had used it against King Pellam, he had destroyed the castle and everything else for miles around. The fields and woods near the castle were burning. The villages and towns looked as if there had been a war. Nothing would grow again in
30 that land for a long time, and the people would be very poor. King Pellam would not be well again for many years.

Merlin found Balin a good horse, for his own was dead. He told him to leave and ride out of that country
35 quickly.

The knight on the island

Balin rode through the forest. Three days later, he saw a castle in front of him. He came to a cross by the road. Letters of gold were written on it. They said:

'NO KNIGHT SHOULD RIDE TO THIS CASTLE   5 ALONE.'

As he read the words, he heard the sound of a hunter blowing his horn not far away. Someone had killed a deer. 'That horn,' thought Balin, 'should be blown for me. I feel that I am the one who will be hunted and   10 killed.'

Then he heard the sound of many voices. A hundred ladies and many knights came from the castle to welcome him. They led him inside. There they gave him food and clean clothes. There was dancing and   15 music. Everything was done to please Balin, the knight who rode to the castle alone.

Then the great lady of the castle came to him and said, 'Knight of the Two Swords, tomorrow you must joust. You must fight with a knight dressed all in red.   20 He is on an island not far from here. No knight may come to this castle without fighting him.'

The lady gave Balin a shield, which she said was better than his own. So the next day, Balin took the shield and left the castle. He rode along the side of a   25 river. Soon he reached an island. He found a large boat tied to the river bank, and rowed himself and his horse across.

When he reached the island, he saw a knight riding towards him. His armour was red. Balin quickly got on   30 his own horse, and turned to face the knight. The two knights lowered their spears and charged. They came together so hard and so fast that both men fell to the ground.

Balin heard a strange noise. He looked up. There, on top of the walls of the castle, and on its towers, were many ladies and knights. They were all watching the battle. The noise he had heard was the noise of their voices.

Balin and the red knight began to fight on foot. They wounded each other badly, but that did not stop them. Again and again they attacked each other until the green grass there was blood red. Just one of their wounds would have been enough to kill the biggest man in the world.

At last the knight in red stopped. He could fight no longer. Balin stopped too. They were both so badly wounded they knew they were near to death.

Then Balin said, 'Who are you? Until now I have never found anyone who could fight so well.'

'My name is Balan,' said the knight. 'I am brother to the good knight, Balin.'

'Oh Balan, my brother,' cried Balin, 'we have killed each other.' Then Balin looked to see which sword he was using. It was the one he had taken from the lady at King Arthur's court. 'With that sword you will kill the person you most love in the world,' the lady had told him.

'I saw you had two swords,' cried Balan, 'but because you had another shield, I thought you were another knight.'

Then the lady came with some of her people. Balan told her that he and Balan were brothers. He asked her to bury them together. Weeping for pity, she agreed to do as he asked. Soon afterwards both Balin and Balan died.

The next day Merlin came. He took Balin's sword — the one Balin had taken from the lady. Using his magic powers, he set it in a marble stone in the river.

The marble stone itself was magic. It was large and heavy, yet it floated on the water. Slowly it floated down the river, until, many years later, it came to Camelot.

After he had done his work, Merlin left the castle and walked into the forest. There, among the lakes, green woods and dark hills, he disappeared. He was never seen again.

Sir Launcelot and Sir Turquin

Sir Launcelot and Sir Lionel search for adventure

One day, two knights from King Arthur's court rode out of a dark forest into a large, open plain. They were
5 Sir Launcelot and his brother, Sir Lionel. They were looking for an adventure, to see how brave they were.

The weather was hot. About midday, Sir Launcelot began to feel sleepy. He noticed a great apple tree, with many smaller trees standing around it. 'Look,' he said,
10 'we can rest under those shady trees for a while.'

They stopped under the trees. Sir Launcelot lay down under the apple tree, put his helmet under his head, and closed his eyes. Sir Lionel kept watch while Sir Launcelot slept.

15 Soon afterwards Sir Lionel saw three knights go riding across the plain. They were going as fast as they could. They seemed to be frightened of something. Then another knight appeared, chasing after them. When Sir Lionel saw him, he thought he had not seen so great
20 a knight before. He had never seen one that rode so well.

As Sir Lionel watched, the strong knight rode up to one of the others, and hit him. With one blow he knocked the man off his horse. The man fell down onto
25 the cold earth, and lay there unmoving. Then the strong knight rode to the next, and did the same to him. After that he went on to the third. When all three were down, he got off his horse, and tied them all up.

Sir Lionel saw this and thought he should fight the great knight. This was the adventure he had been looking for. If he could defeat such a strong knight, he would know he was a good fighter. Very quietly he got himself ready. He was careful not to wake up Sir Launcelot.

Sir Lionel then rode up to the strong knight, and commanded him to turn and fight. The strong knight turned, and immediately hit Sir Lionel so hard that both Sir Lionel and his horse fell down. The strong knight then tied up Sir Lionel and threw him onto his horse. Then, with his four prisoners, he rode away into the forest.

At Turquin's castle

Sir Launcelot knew nothing of this. He woke up long afterwards. He wondered where Sir Lionel had gone. He got on his horse, and went looking for him. After he had ridden a short way, he met a lady riding a small white horse.

Sir Launcelot asked her if she had seen his brother. He said he thought he might have ridden off looking for an adventure.

'Well,' said the lady, 'if he went looking for adventure, he would not need to go very far. I can show you where you will find adventure, if that is what you really want.'

'Why not?' said Sir Launcelot. 'That is why I came.'

'I shall take you to the strongest knight you ever saw,' said the lady. 'His castle is not far from here. If you cannot beat him, I would think no one can. His name is Sir Turquin. In his castle he has sixty-four good knights from Arthur's court. They are his prisoners. I think your brother must be one of them.'

Then the lady led
Sir Launcelot into the forest,
along the side of a river. After
a while they could see a castle. They
5 came to a place near the castle where the river
was not so deep. The water ran noisily over the sand
and stones of the river bed. A large old tree stood there.
Hanging on the tree were many shields.

Sir Launcelot looked at the shapes on the shields, and
10 the different colours. He could see that many of them
had been taken from King Arthur's men. One was his
brother's. Also hanging from the tree was a large round
piece of metal — a gong.

'You will have to fight Sir Turquin before you can set
15 your brother free,' the lady said. 'Hit the gong three
times, and Sir Turquin will come.' Then she rode away
into the forest.

Sir Launcelot first let his horse drink from the river.
Then he hit the gong three times with the handle of his
20 spear. The gong made a great noise, but no one came.
He hit the gong three more times. Still nothing. He hit
it again, and again and again, and kept hitting it with
all his strength until he made a hole in it. Still no one
came.

The great battle

Then Sir Launcelot saw a great knight riding towards the castle. With him, lying across the back of a second horse, lay an armed knight. His hands and feet were tied. Sir Launcelot saw that the prisoner was Gaheris, 5 brother of Sir Gawain.

'Now, fair knight,' Sir Launcelot called out, 'put your prisoner off his horse. Let him rest while we see which of us is the strongest. I have heard you have done great harm to the Knights of the Round Table.' 10

'If you are one of them,' said Turquin, 'then I can tell you I hate you, and all your fellows.'

They lowered their spears and came together as fast as their horses could run. Each man hit the other other in the middle of his shield with great power. The backs 15 of both horses broke, and men and animals fell to the ground.

As soon as they could get off their horses, they took their shields, drew out their swords, and came together eagerly. They hit at each other bravely, with many 20 strong strokes. Soon they both had terrible wounds, and their blood flowed down to the ground. They fought like this for two hours or more, hitting and cutting one another as hard as they could. Then at last they were too tired to fight any more. For a while they stood there, 25 leaning on their swords.

'You are the biggest man I have ever met,' said Sir Turquin. 'You also look like the knight I hate most in this world. If you are not he, I will happily make peace with you.' 30

'Which knight do you hate so much, Sir Turquin?' asked Sir Launcelot.

'His name is Sir Launcelot,' said Sir Turquin. 'I hate him because he killed my brother. If ever I meet that

Launcelot, one of us shall finish off the other, I promise you. Because of him I have killed a hundred good knights. I have wounded a hundred more so badly that they will never fight again. Many more have died in my prison. But I still have sixty-four left. I will give them all to you, if you are not Sir Launcelot.'

'I must tell you the truth,' said Sir Launcelot. 'I am a true Knight of the Round Table, and my name is Launcelot.'

'Then you are most welcome here,' said Sir Turquin. 'We shall not leave until one of us is dead.'

They rushed together again like two wild animals. They smashed at each other with their shields and swords. They fought for another two hours without stopping to rest. Sir Turquin gave Sir Launcelot so many wounds that the ground was covered with blood.

At last Sir Turquin grew tired. For a second he let his shield drop a little. Sir Launcelot immediately jumped at him and knocked him down to his knees. Then, very quickly, he pulled off Sir Turquin's helmet, and cut his head from his shoulders.

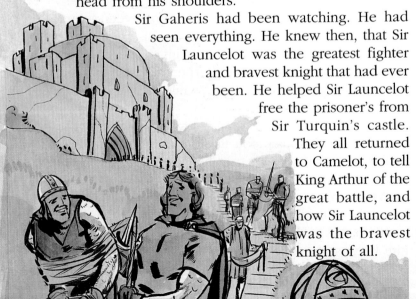

Sir Gaheris had been watching. He had seen everything. He knew then, that Sir Launcelot was the greatest fighter and bravest knight that had ever been. He helped Sir Launcelot free the prisoner's from Sir Turquin's castle. They all returned to Camelot, to tell King Arthur of the great battle, and how Sir Launcelot was the bravest knight of all.

8

A DAY OF MIRACLES

The writing on the Round Table

One year, at the feast of Pentecost at Camelot, something very strange happened to the Round Table. That day, King Arthur, Queen Guenevere, the great lords and their ladies, and all the Knights of the Round Table, went to St Stephen's Church, as was their custom. Afterwards, when they returned to the great hall, the knights saw their names written in gold letters at their places. Every place had been named except one. That was the place they called the Place of Great Danger.

No one ever sat in the Place of Great Danger. In the past a few had tried, but great harm had come to them. Merlin had said only the best knight in all the world could ever take that place, but no one knew who he was yet.

When they looked this time, they saw there was writing at the Place of Great danger too. It said:

'AT PENTECOST, 454 YEARS AFTER THE DEATH OF OUR LORD JESUS CHRIST, THIS PLACE WILL BE FILLED.'

'It seems to me,' said Sir Launcelot, 'that this place will be filled this very day, for today is the feast of Pentecost, and this is the 454th year.' Then he asked for the writing to be covered with a silk cloth, so that
5 only they would know what it said.

As they stood speaking, a servant came in. He said to the king, 'Sir, something marvellous has happened. A great stone has floated down the river, and stopped here at Camelot. I saw a sword sticking in it.'
10 The king was very interested. He and all the knights went down to the river. There they saw a great stone floating on the water. It was of red marble, and stuck in it was a bright, sharp sword. The handle of the sword was made of gold and bright coloured stones, and on
15 it were written these words:

'ONLY THE BEST KNIGHT IN THE WORLD WILL DRAW ME FROM THIS STONE.'

So King Arthur turned to Sir Launcelot. 'Good Sir Launcelot,' he said, 'this sword must be yours. I am
20 sure you are the best knight in the world.'

Then Sir Launcelot answered with a serious look on his face, 'I am sure, sir, it is not mine. I know I am not the best knight in the world, and never was.'

King Arthur then asked Sir Gawain to try to take the
25 sword. He said he would try, but only to please the king. He took the sword by the handle, but could not move it at all. None of the others came forward. They thought if Sir Launcelot would not try, and Sir Gawain could not move it, they would not be able to do any
30 better.

The good young knight

They all returned to the great hall and to their places at the Round Table. But when they had begun their feast, another miracle happened. Suddenly all the doors and windows of the palace blew shut, yet the hall did not seem to be very dark. They were all astonished at this.

Then, into the hall came a very old man, dressed in white. No one knew who he was or where he had come from. With him was a young knight wearing a long red coat. He had no sword or shield, but at his side hung an empty sheath.

Then the old man said to King Arthur. 'Sir, I bring with me a good, brave young knight. He comes from a family of kings. He will bring great honour to the Round Table. Through him, many wonderful things will be done. We have been waiting a long time for him. His name is Galahad.'

Then the old man took the young knight by the hand, and led him through the hall to the Place of Great Danger. He lifted the cloth from the table. The golden writing was still there, but it had changed. Now it said:

'THIS IS THE PLACE OF GALAHAD, THE GOOD PRINCE.'

The king went to Galahad and welcomed him to his court. Then he took the young knight to the river, to show him the great red stone floating in the water.

When Galahad saw the sword in the stone, he put his hand lightly on the handle and drew it out. He slipped it easily into his sheath.

The best knight in all the world had come to Camelot.

The fellowship of good, brave knights

Later that day, when they all sat down to supper, an even greater miracle happened. Just as they were about to begin their meal, they suddenly heard a sharp noise, and then the loud, low rumbling of thunder.

The building shook, as if a great storm had begun. Some of the people began to wonder if the palace would fall down.

Then the hall was suddenly lit up with a marvellous light, seven times brighter than day. Every knight began to look at his neighbours in astonishment, for they all looked younger and stronger than they had ever looked before, and the ladies more beautiful. They sat there in silence. They were too astonished to speak.

Then someone came into the hall carrying something covered with a cloth of white silk. A soft, clear light shone through the cloth. No one in the hall could see what was under the cloth. No one could see clearly who was carrying it. But they all knew that it must be the Holy Grail, the cup used by our Lord Jesus at his last supper. The Holy Grail passed slowly around the hall. Everywhere it went, the air was filled with the sweet smell of beautiful flowers.

Then each knight saw in front of him the food he loved best, but no one wanted to eat. They just sat there, their eyes fixed on the Holy Grail. It was the most wonderful thing they had ever seen. It was the most marvellous thing in the whole world.

When the Holy Grail reached the far end of the great
hall, it moved quickly away, and disappeared. The
bright light got weaker. The Knights of the Round Table
looked at each other. They looked the same as they
had looked before the Holy Grail came into the hall. 5
They found they could speak once more.

Sir Gawain stood up. 'We have seen a great miracle,'
he said. 'We have all been given the food and drink we
love best. But there is one thing we have not received.
We could not see the Holy Grail itself because it was 10
covered up so carefully. Now, in front of you all, I shall
make this promise. From tomorrow, I shall not rest until
I have found the Holy Grail. Until I have seen it with
my own eyes, I shall not return to Camelot.'

The knights listened to Sir Gawain. The words he had 15
spoken were in all their hearts. Without further thought,
they all stood up and made the same promise. They
were astonished at what they had seen. They were
excited about what they would do. The Quest of the
Holy Grail would be the greatest quest there had ever 20
been.

But the king was not pleased. 'You have killed me
with this promise,' he said to Sir Gawain. 'Here, for a
few hours, the Round Table was complete. Here sat the
best fellowship of good, honourable knights that were 25
ever seen anywhere in the world. They came together,
all 150 of them, for just a short while. Now they will
all leave. Many, I am sure, will never meet again in this
world. Many will die on this quest. It fills me with
sorrow to see the fellowship broken up, for I have 30
loved these good knights as well as my life.'

But nothing could be done to stop the knights from
leaving. No knight can break a promise, once he has
made it in front of other knights.

THE TWO ROADS

The white shield

The next morning, all the Knights of the Round Table left Camelot to search for the Holy Grail. They rode off in different directions. One man went this way, another that, for no one knew exactly where the Holy Grail would be. They thought they would trust in God to lead them to it. They were ready for any adventure that might happen.

Sir Galahad left, too. The king and queen gave him some beautiful armour to wear, a fine helmet, and a spear. He also had the sword which he had drawn from the stone. But he had no shield. The king asked him to take a shield, but he refused.

The young knight rode through the forest for four days. He met no one, and nothing happened to him. In the evening of the fourth day, he came to an abbey. The people there greeted him. They took him to a room where they helped him out of his armour. There he found another of the Knights of the Round Table — Sir Bagdemagus.

Sir Galahad asked the other knight why he was there. Sir Bagdemagus said he had heard there was a strange shield in the abbey. People thought that anyone who used it would be killed in less than three days, or so badly wounded he would never fight again.

'Tomorrow I shall take it,' said Sir Bagdemagus. 'I want to see if what they say is true.' Then he looked at Sir Galahad and added, 'If anything bad happens to me, then you should try. I am sure the shield will do you no harm.' Sir Galahad needed a shield. He agreed to wait.

The following morning, Sir Bagdemagus asked the people at the abbey where the shield was. A monk took him into a small church. There, on the wall behind the altar, hung a shield. It was as white as snow, and had a red cross painted on it.

5

'Sir,' said the monk. 'That shield should only be used by the best knight in the world. I do not think you should touch it.'

'Well,' said Sir Bagdemagus, 'I know I am not the best knight in the world, but I shall try to use it all the same.' He took the shield down from the wall. As he left the abbey, he said to Sir Galahad, 'Wait here, until you have heard from me.'

Then Sir Bagdemagus rode away into the forest. He took a young man with him. If anything happened, the young man would come back and tell Sir Galahad.

When they had ridden about two miles into the forest, Sir Bagdemagus and the young man came to a beautiful valley. There they saw a knight coming towards them. He was dressed completely in white. His sword, spear and shield were white, and so was his horse. The knight lowered his spear. He made his horse run forward, as fast as it could go.

Sir Bagdemagus charged towards the white knight, too, and lowered his spear. He hit the white knight's shield, and the spear broke. The white knight hit Sir Bagdemagus so hard that his armour broke away. His spear wounded Sir Bagdemagus in the shoulder.

Sir Melias

The knight got off his horse. He took the strange shield from Sir Bagdemagus. 'You have done yourself great harm, sir,' the white knight said. 'This shield should only be used by the knight who is better than all other knights in this world.'

He turned to the young man. 'Take this shield to the good knight Sir Galahad,' he said. 'It was made many hundreds of years ago, in the Holy city of Sarras. The man who brought it to Britain said long ago that it should be used by Sir Galahad, and no one else.' Then the white knight got back on his horse, and disappeared into the forest.

The young man helped Sir Bagdemagus back to the abbey. He told Sir Galahad about what had happened, and gave him the white shield. Sir Bagdemagus was badly wounded. It would be a long time before he would be well again. The monks in the abbey said they would look after him.

The young man thought about what the white knight had said. He knew Sir Galahad was special. He wanted to ride with him. He wanted to see Sir Galahad's adventures. He went to talk to Sir Galahad. He knelt down at his feet.

'Sir,' he said. 'My name is Melias. I am a king's son. I have come to ask that you make me a knight. Let me ride with you in your quest for the Holy Grail.'

Sir Galahad knew the young man came from a good family. He agreed that he should be a knight. Praying to God, Sir Galahad drew out his sword, and with it he touched the young man gently on each shoulder. 'Sir Melias,' he said, 'may God make you a good knight, and a shining example of how a knight should behave.'

When Sir Galahad left the abbey the next morning, Sir Melias rode with him.

Pride and greed

Sir Galahad and Sir Melias rode through the forest. They
5 came to a place where there was a stone cross, with some writing on it. It said:

'THERE ARE TWO ROADS HERE, ONE TO THE RIGHT, ONE TO THE LEFT. CHOOSE THE ONE YOU WISH TO TAKE. THE ONE TO THE LEFT LEADS TO
10 DANGER AND ADVENTURE.'

'I will take the road to the left,' said Sir Melias. He wanted to see how brave he was. Without waiting to listen to what Sir Galahad thought, he rode off.

He rode for two days without anything happening.
15 Then he came to a large open field. He saw a fine building there — the kind of place where a king might stay when he went hunting. There was a chair outside. On the grass in front of the building, someone had been getting a feast ready. They had placed many good
20 things to eat and drink on some bright-coloured cloths. But Sir Melias took no notice of the food. He had seen something else that interested him much more. There, on the chair, was a golden crown.

He went up to the chair, leant down, took the crown
25 and rode away. He did not get far. A knight came from the building and immediately attacked Sir Melias with his sword. Sir Melias fell to the ground, badly wounded. He could not move.

Just then, Sir Galahad rode out from the trees. He
30 looked down at Sir Melias. 'Ah, Sir Melias, you chose the wrong road,' he said. Sir Galahad then charged towards the knight, and hit him with his spear so hard that it went through his shoulder. Another knight then

came out of the forest and hit Sir Galahad. Sir Galahad drew his sword. He wounded the second knight in the arm, and chased him away.

Then Sir Galahad gently picked up Sir Melias, and took him back to the abbey.   5

An old monk who had once been a knight, took care of Sir Melias. 'The wound is serious,' the old monk said, 'but he will live.'

Then he took Sir Galahad to one side, and spoke very gently to him. 'Sir Melias was wounded because 10 he behaved shamefully,' he said. 'The two roads were the two different ways we can choose in our lives, the good, and the bad. The way to the right is the way of good, honest men. The way to the left is the way of wickedness. Sir Melias chose the bad way.   15

'Sir Melias was proud, so he put himself in danger,' the old monk continued. 'He was greedy, so he took what did not belong to him. These are not things that a good knight should do. And the two knights you fought with in the forest were not men. They were the 20 sins of Sir Melias — the sins of pride and greed. They could not fight against you, Sir Galahad, because you have no pride or greed. You have chosen the good way. That is why you are the best knight in all the world.'

SIR GALAHAD,
KNIGHT OF THE GRAIL

The perfect knight

The Knights of the Round Table were good, brave knights. They were better than other knights, and they were much better than most ordinary men. But they were still full of sin.

Many of them were proud, strong fighters. They were merciful when their enemies asked for mercy. They helped one another, and those in need. But often they killed and wounded others for no good reason.

Sometimes, too, the Knights of the Round Table argued among themselves. They had jousts and fights and battles just as if they were enemies. Sometimes good friends and even brothers fought. Some, like Balin and Balan, killed each other by mistake.

The Knights of the Round Table were not perfect, except for one of them — Sir Galahad. Sir Galahad was the bright, shining star of the Round Table. He had never done anything wrong in his life, and he never would. He was the true, good knight. None better than him had ever lived.

Because he was the perfect knight, there were some things only Sir Galahad could do. There were many evil things in the land, and he was the only one who could set them right.

As he went from place to place in his journeys, people asked him to help them. They took him to places where strange, evil things lived. They showed him wells and rivers where the water boiled and burnt.

They took him to churches where terrible noises came from old graves. In all those places, Galahad, because he was good, chased away the evil. He set things right again.

People had waited for the perfect knight for a long time. They knew one day he would come and save them from evil. They had been waiting for Sir Galahad. Some knew that only the perfect knight, Sir Galahad, would succeed in the most perfect quest of all — the Quest of the Holy Grail.

The broken sword

After many adventures, Sir Galahad came to the waste lands. Nothing grew there because of what Balin had done at Castle Carbonek a long time ago. Sir Galahad rode through the forests of dead trees, and the empty fields, and the burnt villages and towns. He met two other Knights of the Round Table, Sir Percival and then Sir Bors. The three were very happy to see one another again. Slowly they made their way to Castle Carbonek.

When they entered the castle, there was great joy. The people there knew, when Galahad came, that the Quest of the Holy Grail would succeed.

Then King Pellam's son, Eliazar, brought out a broken sword. It was hundreds of years old, and very special. 'Long ago,' he said, 'a great man brought this sword to Britain from the Holy Land. He said it would be mended by the Knight of the Grail.'

Eliazar gave the broken pieces to Sir Bors. Sir Bors held them in his hands, and pushed them together as if to join them. Nothing happened. He gave them to Sir Percival. Sir Percival was no more successful than Sir Bors.

'Now you try,' Sir Percival said as he turned to
Sir Galahad, handing him the pieces. 'If it can be done
by anyone, I am sure you can do it.'

Then Sir Galahad took the pieces and set them
together. In front of all their eyes, the broken pieces
joined themselves. The sword looked as if it had never
been broken. It looked as new and as beautiful as the
day it was first made.

Then when they all saw what Sir Galahad had done,
they knew he was the Knight of the Grail.

An astonishing sight

Suddenly they heard a voice, but they could not see
who spoke. The voice said, 'It is time for the knights
to eat.' The knights were taken to a hall where they
saw a golden table set on silver legs.

Four ladies came into the hall. They were carrying a
small bed. In the bed lay an old man. He had a gold
crown on his head.

The ladies set the bed down in the middle of the hall,
and the king lifted up his head a little. He said, 'Welcome
to Castle Carbonek, Sir Galahad. I have been waiting a
long time for you to come. Balin, the Knight of the Two
Swords, wounded me badly when he came here. I have
been in great pain ever since.' It was King Pellam.

Galahad went to King Pellam. He placed his hands
on his wounds. The king got out of his bed. He stood
up, and began to walk around. Slowly his face filled
with joy and thankfulness. He was not in pain any
more.

Suddenly they all heard the voice again. It said,
'Those of you here who are not on the Quest of the
Holy Grail must leave.' Everyone left the hall except
Sir Galahad, Sir Percival and Sir Bors.

Then the three knights
saw a strange sight. It seemed
that a man came in, carried on a
chair by four angels. He was dressed like
a bishop, and carried a cross in his hand. The angels
set him down in the hall, in front of the golden table.

'I am Joseph,' the man said. 'I was the first Christian
bishop in Britain. I came here from the Holy City, called
Sarras.'

Then the knights were astonished. They knew that 10
the bishop had been dead for more than 300 years.

Then they saw four more angels. Two carried lights,
one carried something under a silk cloth, and the fourth
carried a spear with strange writing on it. It was the
spear Balin had used. The angels placed all these things 15
on the table.

Then, as the knights looked, they saw something
even more astonishing. Something began to give out a
soft, gentle light from under the silk cloth. The room
filled with a sweet smell of beautiful flowers. There, 20
before their very eyes at last, Sir Galahad, Sir Percival
and Sir Bors together saw the Holy Grail. They fell to
their knees, and thanked God.

Then the bishop came and spoke to Galahad. 'Now,' he said, 'you have seen what you most want to see, but you have not yet seen it uncovered. The quest is not yet finished. You are the Knight of the Grail. You must now go from here and take this Holy Grail to the City of Sarras. Tomorrow, go to the sea shore. You will find a ship waiting for you there. Take the sword with you that you got from the marble stone. Sir Percival and Sir Bors will go with you to help you, but no one else. The Holy Grail and the Knight of the Grail must leave this land. They will never come back.'

The knights return

A year or more after this, a knight rode into Camelot, tired and dusty from a long journey. It was Sir Bors. He went to the great hall. Most of the places at the Round Table were empty.

Then Sir Bors told the king and queen how the quest of the Holy Grail had succeeded. He told them all about Sir Galahad's adventures, of his journey across the sea, and what happened to him in the Holy City of Sarras. He told them how Sir Galahad had died when praying to God, and many angels carried his soul up to heaven. He told them how, soon after that, a hand came down and took the Grail itself back to heaven. Sir Percival had died in Saras, too.

The king was sad to hear of the death of the good knight Sir Galahad, and of Sir Percival, but he was full of joy that the quest had succeeded. He then ordered his servants to write down all the adventures of the Holy Grail in a great book. From that time on, the book was kept at the abbey at Salisbury.

The news of what Sir Galahad had done spread through the land. One by one, the knights who had gone on the quest returned to Camelot.

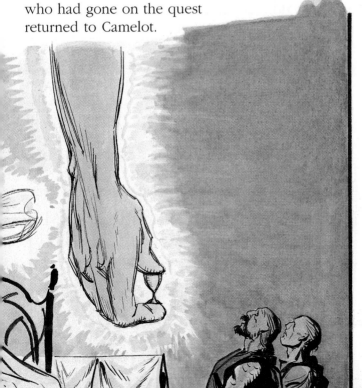

THE WICKED SIR MORDRED

Sir Launcelot and his enemies

All the time he was at the court of King Arthur, Sir Launcelot had loved Queen Guenevere. Their love had been good, and honest, and honourable. But Sir Launcelot's enemies told King Arthur about it, and tried to turn his heart against Sir Launcelot.

The worst of these enemies was Mordred. Mordred was King Arthur's son. He did not honour or respect his father. He hated the good brave knights who loved the king. Most of all, he hated Sir Launcelot.

One day, Mordred and some others came to the king's room. They told him that Launcelot was with the queen. The king ordered them to go to the queen's room and take Sir Launcelot prisoner.

Fourteen armed knights, led by Sir Mordred, went to get Sir Launcelot. They banged on the door loudly. When Sir Launcelot knew why they had come, he looked around for some armour. There was none in the queen's room. Then he wound his coat round his arm,

and opened the door a little. One knight rushed in; but
when he was through, Launcelot closed the door
behind him quickly and locked it. The knight hit out at
Sir Launcelot. Sir Launcelot used his arm with the coat
wound round it to protect himself. He hit back at the   5
knight so hard that he killed him.

Sir Launcelot then took the knight's armour and put
it on himself. When he was ready, he opened the door
of the queen's room, and fought with the other knights.
He killed them all except Sir Mordred. Sir Launcelot   10
then left Camelot. Taking his most trusted followers
with him, he went and hid in the forest not far from
the court.

The king was angry at what had happened. He
thought the queen had stopped loving him. He thought   15
she loved Sir Launcelot instead. The king ordered her
to be burned to death.

On the day when the queen was to go to the fire,
many good knights stood around her. They were not
armed. They wore only long black clothes. They were   20
sad because of what would happen.

Then Sir Launcelot and many others came riding into
Camelot Castle. They attacked the people standing
around the queen. They killed many of them. They set
the queen free. Launcelot took her away with him to   25
his castle, called Joyous Gard.

Mordred makes himself king

King Arthur came to Joyous Gard with his army. There
was a great battle there. During the battle, one of
Sir Launcelot's men knocked the king from his horse.   30
The knight called to Sir Launcelot and asked whether
or not he should kill the king. Sir Launcelot said no.
He saved the king's life.

Sir Launcelot told the king that he did not want there to be a war between them. He hoped there would be peace. He said he would return Queen Guenevere to the king, if he would forgive her. He said he would
5 leave Britain, and go and live in France. King Arthur agreed, and this is what was done. Queen Guenevere returned to Camelot.

But Mordred was not finished with his wickedness. Later, he made more trouble. King Arthur took a great
10 army to France to fight against Sir Launcelot. As soon as the king left Britain, Mordred told everyone that he was dead. Mordred made himself King of Britain. He even wanted to marry Queen Guenevere. He thought if Guenevere were his queen, everyone would respect
15 him.

King Arthur heard what had happened. He went back to Britain immediately. At Dover, there was a battle between King Arthur's men and the knights that followed Mordred. At the end of the day, King Arthur's
20 knights won.

Mordred and his followers ran away. They went to the west, to Camlaan. Thousands of knights came from all over the kingdom and joined Mordred there. King Arthur would have to defeat them, or else he
25 would lose his kingdom.

Arthur and his knights went to Camlaan. The king's army was smaller than Mordred's. Sir Gawain told him not to fight the battle until he had more men in his army. King Arthur said he would make peace with
30 Mordred.

The next day, the two armies faced each other on the plain of Camlaan. There were thousands of good knights on either side. They stood in long lines, King Arthur's army on this side of the plain, Mordred's
35 on the other.

The king and Mordred would meet to try to make peace. They would meet in the open ground between the armies. Everyone would be able to see them there. Mordred would take twelve men with him, and so would King Arthur.

Before he went, King Arthur told his army to watch carefully. He said if none of Mordred's men drew a sword, everything would be well. But if a sword was drawn, then the battle should begin immediately.

Mordred said the same thing to his followers. He said if any of King Arthur's men drew his sword, the battle should begin.

How a snake destroyed a kingdom

King Arthur and Mordred spoke to one another. King Arthur said that Mordred could be lord of the west of the kingdom. Arthur promised that after his death, Mordred would become King of Britain. Everything was agreed. There would be peace.

Then a small but terrible thing happened. A little snake bit the foot of one of the knights standing near the king and Mordred. The pain was great. The man looked down to see what had caused it. He saw the snake. He took out his sword to kill it.

All the soldiers in King Arthur's army saw one of the knights near their king draw out his sword. All the soldiers in Mordred's army saw it too. Both armies then obeyed the command of their leaders — if a sword was drawn, the battle would start.

No one wanted the battle. The king and Mordred had made peace. But now thousands of knights were rushing towards one another. Nothing could be done to stop them. It was the worst battle that ever happened, and it began by accident.

The battle was long and hard. Everywhere good knights fought, pushing and hitting and cutting at one another. The noise of men shouting and horses screaming was terrible. Before long the earth was covered with the blood of the wounded and the dying. All around, dust and dirt flew up into the air. The sky grew dark. After a while no one could see very far. On all sides, men were falling to the ground. One after the other, the Knights of the Round Table fell and died.

That day, 100,000 men were killed. At the end, not a single man in Mordred's army remained alive, except for Mordred himself. He was badly wounded. On Arthur's side only Arthur remained, and two Knights of the Round Table — Sir Bedevere and Sir Lucan.

When King Arthur saw Mordred still standing and alive, his anger became too great. Because of Mordred his kingdom was destroyed. Because of Mordred, he had lost the love of the best of all knights, and of his queen, the gentle Guenevere. Because of Mordred, the fine fellowship of the Round Table had fallen, and would never rise again. The king took up a great sharp spear that was lying on the ground near him. He pointed it at Mordred and rushed towards him. He struck Mordred a terrible blow. The spear went right through him.

But Mordred did not die immediately. When he saw what had happened, he knew he had only minutes to live. In terrible pain, he pulled himself along the spear, closer and closer towards Arthur. When they were face to face, Mordred lifted his sword high in the air. With the last of his strength, he brought it down in one great stroke on the head of the king.

Sir Bedevere and Sir Lucan ran to help the king, but it was too late. Mordred's stroke had cut through the king's helmet. It had wounded him badly. Blood flowed from the king's head and could not be stopped. The two knights knew that the king would soon die.

THE DEATH OF KING ARTHUR

A terrible sight

Sir Lucan and Sir Bedevere held on to the king. They led him between them to a little church not far from the side of a dark lake. When the king was there, he
5 rested for a while. Then, in the distance, they heard the sound of many people shouting and screaming.

'Sir Lucan,' said the king, 'go and see what that noise is about.'

Sir Lucan went out slowly, for he was badly wounded
10 himself. It was by then night time. He had to look hard through the darkness to see what was happening. The moon came out from behind a cloud.

There, on the battlefield, Sir Lucan saw a sight that made his blood run cold. Hundreds of men and women
15 were hurrying about here and there, robbing the dead knights of their jewellery and rich armour. Any knight they found who was not already dead, they killed. They were fighting and arguing among themselves as they did their terrible work.

When Sir Lucan understood this, he came back to the king as quickly as he could. He told him what he had seen.

'Listen to me, my lord Arthur,' he said, 'it would be better if we took you to some town. You will be safer there.'

The king agreed.

The two knights then tried to lift the king, one on each side. However, the king was so badly hurt that he fainted with the pain when they lifted him. Sir Lucan was so badly hurt that he fainted too. Trying to lift the king was too much for him. He fell to the floor and died soon afterwards.

'Alas,' said the king, 'it fills me with sorrow to see this good knight die from trying to help me. He was in more need of help than I was.' Then Sir Bedevere began to weep, for Sir Lucan was his cousin.

'There is no time, yet, for weeping,' said the king, 'for I feel I shall not be in this world much longer. There is something that must be done. Good Sir Bedevere, take my sword, Excalibur, to the lakeside, and throw it far out into the water.'

'I shall do as you ask, my lord,' said Sir Bedevere.

The sword is returned

Sir Bedevere took the sword and went out to the dark lake. As he went along, he looked at the sword. It was a beautiful weapon, covered with bright-coloured stones. He saw that the handle was all gold. He said to himself, 'If I throw this rich sword into the water, it will do no good to anyone. Perhaps the king does not really mean me to throw it away. He hid Excalibur under a tree, and went back.

When he returned, he told the king he had done as he had asked.

'What did you see, when you threw the sword into the lake?' asked the king.

'I just saw the dark waves, and the wind blowing across the water,' Sir Bedevere answered.

'You are not telling me the truth,' said the king. 'Please go again, and do as I asked.'

Sir Bedevere went back to the tree and picked up the sword. He still thought it was a sin and a shame to throw away such a beautiful thing. Once more, he hid it and returned.

'What did you see at the lake?' asked the king again.

'Sir,' said Sir Bedevere, 'I saw the waves washing over the rocks, and the moonlight dancing on the water.'

'That is still not the truth,' said King Arthur angrily. 'Now you have disobeyed me twice. Who would have thought that such a good knight, and one I loved so well, would try to take my rich sword.'

Sir Bedevere went out again. This time he took hold of the sword and walked down to the lakeside. The night sky was now clear. The moon shone brightly and he could see all around. Sir Bedevere took one last look at the beautiful weapon. Then he threw the sword as far out over the water as he could.

What happened next astonished and frightened him.
He had thought the sword would fall into the water and
sink. He watched it fly through the air, and begin to
fall towards the lake. Just as it was about to touch the
water, however, an arm suddenly came up. The hand 5
on the arm caught the sword by the handle. It held the
sword straight up so that it shone and glittered
in the moonlight. Then, after waving the
sword backwards and forwards
three times, the arm, and
the sword, slowly sank
down below the
waves.

Sir Bedevere ran back to the king and told him what
had happened.

'Now I know you have obeyed me,' said the king.
'And now, Sir Bedevere, I must ask you to take me to
5   the lake. I fear I have waited here too long.'

The ship by the lake

At the waterside, they found a ship waiting. In it were
many fair ladies. Three of them were queens. They
were all dressed in black clothes and their heads were
10 covered. They wept and cried out loudly when they
saw Sir Bedevere carrying King Arthur to them.

'Put me in the ship,' said the king.

Gently Sir Bedevere lifted the king into the ship.
There the three queens took him in their arms. Full of
15 sorrow, they set him down on soft pillows, and sat
around, crying. One of the queens said, 'Ah, dear
brother, why have you stayed away from me so long?'

Then the sailors began to row, and the ship moved
slowly away from the land.

20 When Sir Bedevere saw they were going without
him, he cried out, 'My lord Arthur, what shall I do? How
can you leave me here alone among my enemies?'

'Do not be sad, good Sir Bedevere,' said the king
gently. 'Everything will be well. Do not put your trust
25 in me any longer. There is nothing in me for you to
trust. I must return to where I belong. I must go to the
land of Avalon, the land of dreams. If you hear no more
of me, pray to God for my soul.'

All that time the queens and ladies wept. They cried
30 out so much that Sir Bedevere's heart almost broke with
pity. He watched them go, slowly across the lake,
further and further away into the darkness. They were
leaving him alone in this world of pain and trouble.

When, at last, he lost sight of the ship, tears fell from his eyes like rain. Slowly he walked away into the forest.

The next morning, when it got light, he saw he had reached a small church. Gladly he went inside to rest. Inside he found an old holy man, a monk. He was lying on the ground, praying. Close by was a grave that had been dug that night.

'Sir, who is buried here?' he asked.

'Fair son, I do not know for sure,' the monk replied. 'But not long ago some ladies came. They brought with them a dead knight. They asked me to bury him.'

'Alas,' said Sir Bedevere, 'that must have been my good, kind lord, King Arthur.'

Then Sir Bedevere asked the monk to let him stay there. 'I will never leave this place for the rest of my life,' he said. 'I shall stay here and pray to God for the soul of my good King Arthur, and for his marvellous fellowship of brave knights.'

QUESTIONS AND ACTIVITIES

CHAPTER 1

Use these words to fill in the gaps: **altar, anvil, king, lords, marble, prayers, steel, strange, stuck, writing.**

When the (1) _____ were finished, the people saw something (2) _____. Near the high (3) _____ stood a great stone. It was of bright, white (4) _____. In the centre was a large, heavy (5) _____ of grey (6) _____ with a sharp sword stuck in it. The sword had gold (7) _____ on it. It said the man who could pull out the sword was the true (8) _____ of all the land. Some great (9) _____ tried to pull it out, but not one of them could. It was (10) _____ fast.

CHAPTER 2

Some of these sentences are true and some are false. Which ones are true, and what is wrong with the false ones?

1 Sir Ector could not pull the sword from the stone.
2 Arthur and Sir Ector knelt down in front of Sir Kay.
3 Sir Ector said he was Arthur's father.
4 The Bishop was surprised because Arthur was so old.
5 Merlin said Arthur was the father of Uther Pendragon.

CHAPTER 3

Put the words at the end of these sentences in the right order.

1 Arthur's sword broke ...   [he] [knight] [when] [the] [fought].
2 Merlin made the knight ...   [deep] [into] [sleep] [a] [fall].
3 Merlin and Arthur ...   [a] [to] [lake] [wide] [rode].
4 Arthur was surprised ...   [and] [cold] [blood] [his] [ran].
5 In the lake an arm ...   [water] [had] [from] [risen] [the].
6 In its hand ...   [shining] [was] [bright] [a] [sword].

CHAPTER 4

There are twelve mistakes in this paragraph. Can you find them?

Gawain and Gaheris rode after the red deer. From the noise of the wind, they knew which way to go. They came to a bridge. Gawain noticed a short knight sitting on the other side. The knight said Gawain had to talk with him. Gawain and Gaheris soon left the other side. Then Gawain and the other horse rode towards one another as slowly as they could. Gawain knocked the knight off his chair.

CHAPTER 5

Put the letters of these words in the right order.

The Lady of the Lake came to (1) **toruc**. She asked for Balin's head. Balin (2) **mailedytime** knew her. She was an (3) **crenasthens** who had killed Balin's (4) **trehom.** For three years, Balin had been (5) **cregishan** for her to (6) **snuhip** her. Balin took out his (7) **wrods** and cut off the lady's head.

CHAPTER 6

Put these sentences in the right order. The first one is done for you.

1 Balin heard that King Pellam was going to give a feast.
2 Balin came to a tower and climbed up the stairs.
3 Balin drew out his sword and killed Garlon.
4 The castle began to shake, and the walls broke and fell.
5 Garlon hit Balin across the face for staring at him.
6 King Pellam attacked Balin with a great battleaxe.
7 He picked up a spear and threw it straight at the king.

CHAPTER 7

Choose the right words in these notes about Sir Turquin.

The knight Turquin (1) **loved/hated** most in the (2) **palace/world** was (3) **Launcelot/Gawain**. He had killed Turquin's (4) **brother/sister**. Because of that, Turquin had killed a (5) **thousand/hundred** good (6) **knights/kings**.

CHAPTER 8

Put the notes about these people in the right boxes.

1 Sir Galahad	(a)	did not want the knights to go on the quest.
2 Sir Gawain	(b)	sat in the Place of Great Danger.
3 King Arthur	(c)	wanted to see the Holy Grail.

CHAPTER 9

Who said this? Choose from: **Sir Bagdemagus, the white knight, Sir Melias, Sir Galahad, the old monk.**

1 'May God make you a good knight.'
2 'Let me ride with you in your quest for the Holy Grail.'
3 'The way to the right is the way of good, honest men.'
4 'I know I am not the best knight in the world.'
5 'You have done yourself great harm, sir.'

CHAPTER 10

Put the underlined sentences in the right paragraphs.

1 Because he was perfect, there were some things that only Sir Galahad could do. <u>Nothing grew there because of what Balin had done.</u> He was the only one who could set them right.

2 After many adventures, Sir Galahad came to the waste lands. <u>However, he was full of joy that the quest had succeeded.</u> He rode through the forests of dead trees.

3 Sir Galahad took the pieces and set them together. <u>There were many evil things in the land.</u> The sword looked as if it had never been broken.

4 The king was sad to hear of the death of Galahad. <u>In front of all their eyes, the broken pieces joined themselves.</u> He ordered his servants to write everything down in a book.

CHAPTER 11

Put the beginnings of these sentences with the right endings.

1 Mordred told the king ...   (a) ... to watch carefully.
2 Launcelot hid in the forest ... (b) ... cut through the king's helmet.
3 Launcelot told the king ...   (c) ... Launcelot was with the queen.
4 King Arthur told his army ...   (d) ... he hoped there would be peace.
5 Because of Mordred ...   (e) ... not far from the court.
6 Mordred's stroke ...   (f) ... the Round Table had fallen.

CHAPTER 12

Write the right answers. Choose from: **grave, church, Bedevere, bury, battlefield, jewellery, Lucan, black.** *The name of a beautiful weapon will appear in the centre.*

(1) _____ threw the king's sword into the lake. (2) _____ died trying to lift the king. (3) A dead person might be placed in a _____. (4) People robbed the dead knights of their _____. (5) On the _____, Sir Lucan saw a sight that made his blood run cold. (6) The queens in the ship wore _____ clothes. (7) A monk was praying in a _____. (8) Some ladies asked the monk to _____ the dead knight.

Oxford
Progressive
English Readers

GRADE 1

Alice's Adventures in Wonderland
Lewis Carroll

The Call of the Wild and Other Stories
Jack London

Emma
Jane Austen

The Golden Goose and Other Stories
Retold by David Foulds

Jane Eyre
Charlotte Brontë

Just So Stories
Rudyard Kipling

Little Women
Louisa M. Alcott

The Lost Umbrella of Kim Chu
Eleanor Estes

The Secret Garden
Frances Hodgson Burnett

Tales From the Arabian Nights
Edited by David Foulds

Treasure Island
Robert Louis Stevenson

The Wizard of Oz
L. Frank Baum

GRADE 2

The Adventures of Sherlock Holmes
Sir Arthur Conan Doyle

A Christmas Carol
Charles Dickens

The Dagger and Wings and Other Father Brown Stories
G.K. Chesterton

The Flying Heads and Other Strange Stories
Edited by David Foulds

The Golden Touch and Other Stories
Edited by David Foulds

Gulliver's Travels — A Voyage to Lilliput
Jonathan Swift

The Jungle Book
Rudyard Kipling

Life Without Katy and Other Stories
O. Henry

Lord Jim
Joseph Conrad

A Midsummer Night's Dream and Other Stories from Shakespeare's Plays
Edited by David Foulds

Oliver Twist
Charles Dickens

The Mill on the Floss
George Eliot

Nicholas Nickleby
Charles Dickens

The Prince and the Pauper
Mark Twain

The Stone Junk and Other Stories
D.H. Howe

Stories from Greek Tragedies
Retold by Kieran McGovern

Stories from Shakespeare's Comedies
Retold by Katherine Mattock

Tales of King Arthur
Retold by David Foulds

The Talking Tree and Other Stories
David McRobbie

Through the Looking Glass
Lewis Carroll

GRADE 3

The Adventures of Huckleberry Finn
Mark Twain

The Adventures of Tom Sawyer
Mark Twain

Around the World in Eighty Days
Jules Verne

The Canterville Ghost and Other Stories
Oscar Wilde

David Copperfield
Charles Dickens

Fog and Other Stories
Bill Lowe

Further Adventures of Sherlock Holmes
Sir Arthur Conan Doyle

Great Expectations
Charles Dickens

Gulliver's Travels — Further Voyages
Jonathan Swift